Eda Saltürk &
Atahan M. Kabaş

Ink and Affection

Poetry

Bibliografische Information der Deutschen Nationalbibliothek: Die Deutsche Nationalbibliothek verzeichnet diese Publikation in der Deutschen Nationalbiografie; detaillierte bibliografische Daten sind im Internet über dnb.dnb.de abrufbar.

Herstellung und Verlag: BoD – Books on Demand, Norderstedt Germany

ISBN: 978-3-7597-3123-4

Expressing your feelings can be hard sometimes, Ink and Affection will help you go through these times with words, metaphors, and rhymes.

<3

Dear reader ...

We both sat down together and drafted poems about many possible situations in life and put ourselves in those perspectives.
Whether grief or being in love or coming to terms with something. We have put ourselves in the shoes of characters we have created and written down the feelings. All these scenarios are mostly fiction but that does not mean that we did not put our hearts and souls into these poems.
We hope the poems will find the people who really need them.
Enjoy a glimpse of the worlds and lovers we have created.
:)

Contents

Leading Light

The sky turns pink, orange, and red,
red, like the rose in your hand.
We are watching the sun set.

My mind says "I love you."
See your eyes ocean blue.
All my worries
I have been thinking about,
just went blackout.

The scent of the rose
rises to my nose.
It smells like the flowers
you first gave me.

The sky is turning blue, grey, and black,
Black like the stones we stacked.
We are watching stars shine bright,
giving us leading light.

Futureless

You
a love, so true,
unknown to you, it makes me wonder,
a future we never share,
leaving me longer,
lost in despair.

Our paths will never intertwine,
so, I keep my moments,
they are forever mine.
Love is nothing we receive,
but joy we shared; I always believe.

My Rose

You are a rose in a field of sunflowers.

Your thorns keep out everyone who is not good for you.
Your soul radiates this love that only I can feel or see.
We have this place for ourselves, only we can enter it.
Only we have the key to it.
We carry the key to our hearts in our souls.
Your thorns do not bother me, because when you're
near me, they are blunt.

Deep Red

Every night when you are around,
there is something bound.
Your eyes seeking me,
even when I am asleep.
Every night when I close my eyes,
I still feel haunted,
but never really wanted.

I open my eyes,
wishing for better days.
Your judging gaze,
I feel it from far away.
I raise my arm and gain,
the horrible reminder of pain.
And a deep red covering the blues.

Phantom Sense

Even though you are not here,
I feel your hand touching mine,
your heart beating with mine,
as if time was not passing by.
Looking through the portal that connects us,
a bond created without touch,
just the phantom sense, thus,
connecting us.

United

The big day has finally come,
the day where you and I unite as one.
The commotion all around,
is louder than any sound.

The scent of kerosene,
makes me feel serene.
It is any minute now,
I have been waiting for so long,
constantly thinking of our vow.
I have even written a love song.
The moment has come.
I have never felt so excited.
Here we are and we become
United.

Love´s Groove

The sun is shining in a golden colour,
you give me all your love,
in this special hour.
Your love makes me move,
makes my heart race,
makes me feel that special groove.
Just when I see your face.
Love´s groove is like the eighty´s,
always feeling weightless.

Or Not

The smiles I see every day,
is what makes me wish I was away.
All those familiar faces glare at me.
Your judgy *eyes,*
your judging *words,*
your judging *lies.*
All you see is the tip of the iceberg.
All your stupid lies and words, lie far behind me.
Though they leave a scar that is inside me.
Once you dive deeper in and see what you have caused,
is what is going to make you feel
sorry for your actions,
or not.
You might enjoy what you have caused but you will
regret it once you realise
the life it cost,
Or not.

Unrequited

I miss the things we never had.
Maybe they are only in my dreams but maybe one day
you will find them deep inside you.

I look at you and I think about things I can never have.
I think about what it would be like if you looked at me
the same way because I don't just look at you once,
not just twice,
not just three times.
You are in my head, in my eyes,
in my heart,
forever.

You would be so well together, they said.
You would make a cute couple, they admitted,
but deep down inside you
there are the words
he will never ask you.

Fighting

Cracks are forming in my heart,
as your voice raises.
I know there is no intention of harm,
as the noise quiets down.
It feels like eternity but your charm,
fixes all the cracks, gone
and healed.
Including a bond,
stronger than ever.

I wish to have you forever.

I can fix him.

I can fix him.
He is the poetry in my eyes.
The words unwritten.
I can fix him.
He is the love's sweet embrace.
I remember, I deserve grace.
I need to open my heart for a love that is real.
A love that sees my worth and makes me feel.
I can fix him.
I am like a gem, a treasure, the only one, so rare.
I do not settle for less, for my heart to repair.
I let my love ignite,
For a person, so right.

But I can fix him.
Really.

I don't deserve her.

I don´t deserve her.
A heart so pure.
She is the one I adore, for what I´m sure.
I see her light, her grace so bright.
She deserves so much better,
a love so right.
I don´t deserve her.
I hope I could be the sunshine after the rain,
with my heart feeling joy and pain.
To be the best I can, to show her love, to be her man.
I aim to be better,
but I don't deserve her.
I doubt myself, for where I stand.
She deserves a love so grand.
My doubts creep in, shadows cast,
can I be the one to make it last?
Am I the one who doesn't deserve her?
I am.
Really.

My Notebook

I counted signals and signs,
as I drove up the road.
I wrote each one down,
rejoicing that I could read them flawlessly,
only to rip them all out at once
and throwing them out of the frosted window of my car.
Just because the traffic lights changed to red
and I had to stop,
stop driving to your heart.

Your Love

I never thought I would chase,
but within all this haze,
your love is special,
like no other.
Stronger than a mother's,
I lose myself in your galaxies,
wishing that time would freeze,
wishing for no other realities.
Just this beautiful spring breeze,
loosing myself in your eyes,
holding your hands tight,
let your lips meet mine,
while you and the stars shine.

I know, but I don't (1)

I know his name.
I know his face.
I know his smile.
I know his eyes.
I know his laugh.
I know the way he writes.
I know the way he talks.
I know his favourite sport.
I know his parents' names.
I know the subjects he likes and dislikes.
I know he has a good heart.
I know everything about him.
but what I do not know is
if in the future
by some miracle
he would like me back.

I know, but I don't (2)

I know her name.
I know her face.
I know her smile.
I know her laugh.
I know the way she talks.
I know her favourite thing to do.
I know her favourite and her least favourite subject.
I know the way she does her hair.
I know she has a good heart.
I know she loves her friends and family.
but what I do not know is
if in the future
by some miracle
I could talk to her.
and tell her,
that I like her.

Just A loner in October

There is nothing more left to cry,
I said it's over.
But my feelings are more than ever before since I'm
older.
I don't know why,
tears run dry.
I think it's not the time to say goodbye.
Just a glimpse of your eye,
every time I look over my shoulder.
The wish I gave in October,
will never come closer.
The dust I see fly,
more and more high.
I'm just the loner,
always sober.
You'll never think "Phone her."
but I want to come closer.
Should I just try?
I did.
And you gave me the *no* after the *why*.

The growing tree

I´m drying,
nothing to come,
so, I kept trying,
trying for love, to get some.

I can´t move,
just waves in the wind,
moveless, hopeless, loveless,
trying to get to the roof.

Like a tree to its roots,
hoping for water,
making it greener,
making it live longer,
and beautiful.

Your Voice

Your voice
A melody to my head.
Your voice
I want to hear until death.
Your voice
every word you´ve said.
Your voice
letters that fled.
Your voice
silent messages I always read.

Note

Be sure that whenever you are not feeling well,
you can always call me.
I will always be there for you.

That Was My Holiday

As I was sitting by the shore,
my throat war feeling sore.
From all the screams I have unleashed,
in the night in which you have tortured me.

Fear struck,
my eyes shut.
It was a dream,
is what I wish it was.

In the end
we all forget,
that this,
this week,
was my holiday.

Two Stones

You´re the aquamarine.
I love your blue perfection.
Could watch you every little second,
look into your beautiful heart.

I´m the opal to you,
transparent with flecks of colour.
My hope does not end,
Hoping one day, turning into sapphire.

The Difference

We love each other,
but believing breaks us apart.
we are like fire and oxygen,
you are the air I need to breathe.
The one who gives me love and security.
I love you.
It breaks me.

Acceptance

I stopped this a long time ago,
but something pulls me back.
Now more than two eyes are looking at you
and I´m caught in the moment between missing and accepting.
I believe in a sign
that you and I are something,
something that was meant to be.
Just that it's not the right time
and there will never be a right one.

My Bright Light

I will love you,
as long as the sun
burns in the sky,
as long as the moon
shines its light,
into the dark night,
until the raging
blue oceans become calm and run dry.
I will love you until
the end of time.
My bright light
in the dark night.

The one who makes it all right.

Who?

Who can restore my thousand lost minutes that I could
have spent with you?
Who can look inside me when it comes to you?
Who can have my love I have for you?
Who can give me the kind of love I lost?

M

Tears of goodbye were even worse when I knew it
would be my last ones you´ll see.
It got worse after I realized you do not know as much as
I did back then.
Everybody knows you.
They take your name into their mouths.
I´m just like you.
Probably because you made the person I am now.
Even without you.

Question Mark

We question a lot of things far too rarely.
If you had not discovered this one thing for yourself,
would you be any different?
If someone important to you was taken out of your life,
would it change anything about you?
Who are really the loyal friends?
And who are we just friends with until the hourglass
drops the last grain of sand?

Your eyes

You know how to keep eye contact, but I fear it because
it is you.
I love your eyes, but I can´t look inside them.
I fear getting lost in them.
I love your eyes.
I just look at you when you do not, so you don't think I
am obsessed with you.
But I am.

Vanished?

I do not know if I am a friend
or a foe
or even something more.
Your eyes speak many languages,
but not mine.
And even when your hand engages
with mine.
I do not know if I only cause you woe,
my heart feels famished.
Is this what I owe?
Is your love … vanished?

All I ever needed

The sweetness of your face.
The tenderness of your warm embrace.
My heart is secured around you,
a beautiful red covering the internal blue.
The feeling of that blue fading,
a great comfort.
Our hearts are trading,
love, making us triumphant.

Only You

I love you and only you,
even though,
we might not think things through.
But hey, that is just what humans do.
I like to think,
that this is part of our life,
the adventurous, questionable,
sometimes,
horrible sides.
But without you,
I will feel another high,
unless,
I lose myself to drugs
another time.

Love Spark (1)

You let our love spark
Lit our torch
Which led us through the dark
I kept trying hard
To fight your darkness
A few nights it fades
It comes and goes
Now I ask you to take my hand
Hold it tightly to our heart
And let this love go in
For our lifetimes

I am just a normal mortal boy
Filled with sparks of life and joy
But around you I feel immortal
Strong, loved and light
I keep falling for you
Over and over again
Never losing a grain
Of feelings

Love Spark (2)

I keep on trying to show you real love
But the darkness takes you away
Takes you down a dark way
Away from my hand
To listen to the dark band
The darkness takes you over
I want to raise your voice
I am wishing for a four-leafed clover
To cover up that noise
To free your hand and engage it with mine
So, both of us can shine

Fight my angel fight
And make this right
I want to make this last
Ant not the last
With this I declare war on darkness
And let our love spark
Since that is what led us through the darkness

Affection

I live in a world full of affection,
where love is a sweet confection.
Emotions are soar, heart adore
but in a blissful connection.
A sanctuary of pure joy, no room for rejection.
Love´s embrace, a sacred place, a divine reflection.

I live in a world, in a realm devoid of affection,
where hearts face disconnection.
Emotions wane, spirits strain, lost in a blank direction,
No joy to find, just a void of imperfection.
Lonely space, barren place, devoid of love´s
resurrection.

Support

In the realm of dreams, where hopes reside,
there are friends who stand by your side.
With unwavering faith and endless cheer,
they lift you up when doubt draws near.
They believe in your vision, your heart´s desire,
fuelling your passion, igniting your fire.

I stopped.

I stopped talking and no one talks back.
I stopped sending and my mailbox stood empty.
No message, for real.
I stopped worrying and no one ever did on his side of my life.
Words wrapped in rose gold with a glimpse of no caring.
Heartbreaking.
Saying "Shut up" but telling me they missed me.
I stopped missing and no one misses back.
"You have no reason to be so mad!"
I stopped keeping it inside me then suddenly all the pieces of me shattered.

The Maze

Longing for you,
that flame won´t fade.
In this hushed moment,
memories cascade,
Echoes of your laughter,
in my head.
A memory of a love
I think about.

Lost in a maze of emotions
untold,
like a ship adrift in waters
cold,
searching for a beacon in the
night,
guiding me back to your
light.

Where Is My Money?

What is this feeling that I am
feeling,
Is it love or faith?
Or am I lying?
Just forget it,
I am dying.

Your heart locked me out,
when I saw what you were about.
Now I hear your whines from far away,
saying,
"Where did you go? Don't you love me enough?

Forget that you are only after one part.
The one part that separates people.
The part which makes them feel like they have achieved
something big.
It is, it is just a currency.
What counts is just the heart.
And all loyalty that lies inside,
Well, nobody cares, where is my money?

The Sunset

There is this something I my head
orange, yellow and red
Somehow, it reminds me of you,
the beautiful, loving and "chaud"
Every time the sun sets,
the orange, yellow and red
reminds me of our debut.
As the couple that would never separate.
I miss you; I really do.
I wish I could revue,
all those days we have spent

I wish that this did not end.

You or Me?

Probably should´ve end it.
I was smarter in the end.
Probably could´ve said the truth,
about your deeds
your lies,
your Claims
You should have let it be.
Stick to the truth.
A lot of things happen, when on mute.
A lot of people can see it.
They save your words.
Mind, head, and more.
But we see each other, more or less.
You are in happiness.
I see your contentment.
But you left our past,
in a huge mess.
But, maybe,
the end would´ve looked different,
maybe if she wasn´t between us,
like a lie between your truths.
I heard it. I saw it. I made it. End.

Your Knight

A beautiful tone in my ears
It is your voice.
As I lose all my fears
You leave me no choice.
My body feels light.
My lips meet yours.
Everything feels right.

I slowly wrap my arms around you,
very tightly.
Feeling your heartbeat,
very lightly.
Watching the starlight shining,
very brightly.
You tell me I am acting,
very knightly.

Heartbreak

I love listening to your voice.
I hate to listen to your heartbreak.
Feeling your heart drown in a lake.
There is only one thing I can do.
Promising you that I would never do,
such a thing to you.
I would never leave your side, never.

You deserve so much better.

Scars

Scars do not come from my enemies.
They come from people I thought would never be one of them.
Scars come from things I have trusted.
With my heart.
But it is like a knife.
If I go a little too far,
It is over.
And the wound won´t close,
if I do not let go.

Loss

Losing someone can be hard.
Getting to know someone new can be enriching. The loss my make you sad at first, but once you realize that the person was taken from you for a reason, you feel much better because you know that the person was not good for you.
The person has made you feel bad in some situations.
The person has given you thoughts that you shouldn´t have.
That is why sometimes it is even good when you lose someone.
That is what make us strong.
Dealing with loss.
In retrospect, you realise that you are so much better without the person.
You also realize that the person is not interested in you, when it comes to situations like the ones that separate people.
Live your life the way you feel the best.

Inadequate

This love is real and true,
I do not know who I would be without you.
I am always thinking of us two.
And all the things we do.
But there is this feeling inside,
deep inside my heart.
That my love
is never enough.
No matter what
you say or proof to me.
I always feel,
inadequate.

Unacquainted

Your face drags me into you,
like a black hole,
chains attached to you and me.
Your smile is precious,
your eyes are too,
God, I wish that I were with you.
I watch every breath you take
and every move you make.
I follow you, to your home,
I watch the place you roam.
I approach you, take your hand,
you look at me, your eyes are stunning.
You look said more than words,
but I did not want to let go.
My vision was tainted,
I get it now, I am unacquainted.

Far, but close

The longing I have,
from this distant love,
we are so far but I feel so close.
My friends are doubting the most,
even with the distance we drove.
Just to be on your behalf.

What is holding all this together?
I cannot choose between either,
to either stay or go.

But I love so.

The End

It was once strong,
slowly turning into grey.
As I am the one feeling I give my all,
each day.
But this needs to be a dance,
a two-way street,
both hearts must share, both must meet.
In the garden of us,
a flower blooms.
Yet one side feels like it is facing gloom.
One half gives, the other takes,
leaving our bond feeling like it breaks.
The thread will never mend,

we have reached our end.

The Manuscript

I am sitting here
Staring at the manuscript of memories
With tears of ink
Ready to be written down
Looking at the words used in the beginning
And compared to the last ones
There is no successful conclusion incoming
Just blank spaces
Never to be filled
Should I just stop authoring the book of us?

Ink and Affection

Unleashed Thoughts

The Last Ink

In the tapestry of life, love is the thread that binds us all. May these poems remind you of the magic and warmth that love brings into our lives. Even if love hurts us all, let love be your guide, your solace, and your joy. With every beat of your heart, may you find love in all its glory.

Even if love and affection seem like a riddle, there is not a single riddle that you cannot solve in this world; poetry might be thou key. So set your thoughts free; you shall feel what you read; your interpretation is as free as love could be.

This way of expression is special to us all; is has guided us since the beginning of time. Let us all write until our inks becomes dry. Let the pen guide your thoughts and express your emotions on paper, so they will last forever. The ancient concept of writing with a quill using ink dates back many years, but that does not mean that we should not keep this tradition up. This ancient way of expression is keeping up till this day, and it expresses all we ever wish to say. Let us be the generation to revive writing poetry. Literature is a particularly important part of our lives, so let us cherish our ability to write texts,

letters and poetry. Cherish the ink, the quill, and the paper as long as it exists.
Our ink is empty now ... We will need substitute ... but what could it possibly be?
A liquid with such honour to be ...
A secret that will be revealed.
...

Blood and Spite

Sometimes love breaks apart in a bad manner.
The ink bleeds.
Your thoughts become inevitable, spite and vengeance will fill your soul.
Your emotions will be chaotic, loud, and toxic, but how do you express this?

~ Eda & Atahan

@edasaltrkautorin
@boredyoshu